DO PENGUINS' FEET FREEZE?

Wild answers to wacky questions from nature!

PUBLISHING

CONTENTS

ARE DOVES AND PIGEONS THE SAME?

Pigeons are a common sight wherever you are – you'll see them in cities and the countryside. But what makes a pigeon a pigeon?

Pigeons belong to a group of birds known as the Columbiformes – a group that includes the extinct dodo (the Raphidae family) and pigeons and doves (the Columbidae family). But what is the difference between pigeons and doves? To be honest, there is no difference. There is no scientific distinction between pigeons and doves. There are over 300 species and they all belong to the same family Columbidae. The only distinction is made in the English language. In other languages all over the world, there is only one word for this group of birds. So, when are you a dove? When you are small, you are a dove, when you are big, you are a pigeon and that is the only difference.

All pigeons and doves make the same crooning or cooing call, and they also make a loud clatter with their wings when they fly away.

The woodpigeon is the largest pigeon in the pigeon family. All pigeons and doves have the same features – small, rounded heads, small, slim bills, rounded bodies with dense, soft feathers and short, scaly legs.

WHERE DO CHICKENS COME FROM?

Chicken is one of the most popular meats in the world. But where does the modern-day chicken come from? The chicken, as we know it nowadays, comes from a wild chicken species – the red junglefowl that lives in Asia.

About 7,000 years ago, people started domesticating red junglefowl – they kept the chickens in captivity and bred them. But they didn't breed the chickens for the meat or for laying eggs. They bred them for cockfighting. So, in fact, only the cock birds (males) were important, and the hens (females) were not used. Chickens started being kept for laying eggs and meat about 2,300 years ago in the Middle East. Now, they are the most important economic livestock we have in the world. There are about 23 billion chickens alive today – more than three chickens per human being!

Male red junglefowl from Southeast Asia (opposite), from which the common brown hen (above) was domesticated.

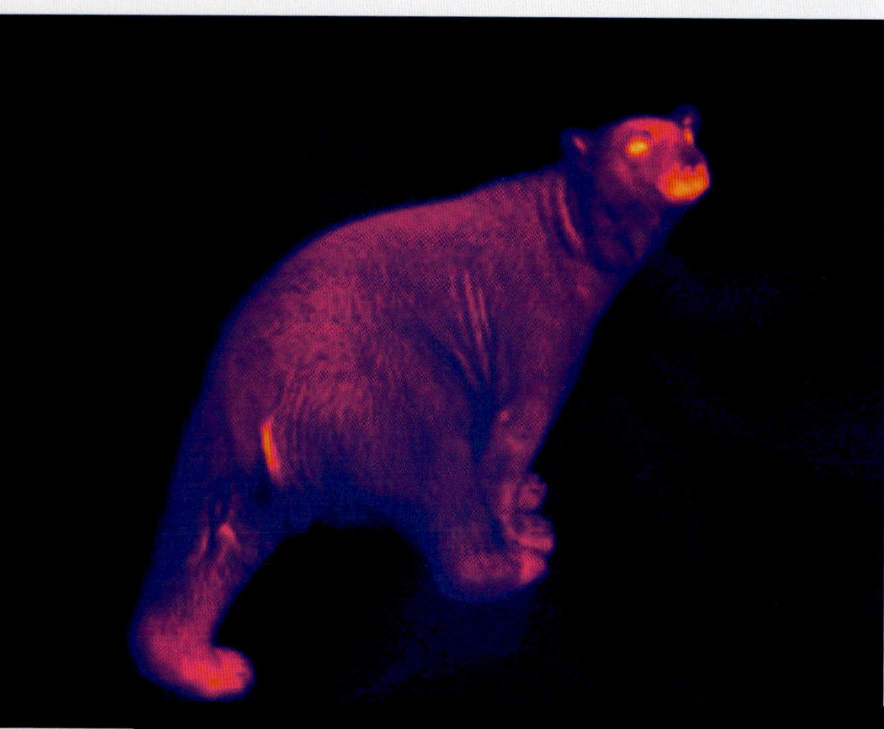

The purple and blue areas of this image, taken with a thermogram, show cool areas and therefore how well the polar bear's thick fur insulates it. The yellow warmer areas show where heat is released.

HOW DO POLAR BEARS STAY WARM?

Living inside the Arctic Circle, polar bears are the largest species of bear alive today. Their white coat is the perfect camouflage. But does it hide other survival tricks?

A cross-section of the hollow centre of a polar bear hair. The hair is also oily so it repels water.

Polar bears appearing white is a fantastic way for them to blend in with their surroundings in the Arctic, so that when they hunt their prey, such as bearded or ringed seals, they can sneak up on them before striking. But the fur is more than just a way to keep them hidden. In fact, a polar bear's fur isn't white at all, it's actually clear. Amazingly, each individual polar bear hair is a transparent hollow tube. This helps trap in heat to keep them nice and warm. Under all their fur they have black skin, which helps them absorb more of this trapped heat and keeps them warm in the ice-cold winds of the Arctic.

WHY DON'T PENGUINS' FEET FREEZE?

How long could you stand in snow with bare feet? Emperor penguins do it for months, so how do they keep their feet warm?

Emperor penguins rock back and forth on their feet to reduce contact with the ground, which helps them keep their feet warm. To prevent their feet from freezing, they maintain a constant temperature using a brilliant countercurrent heat exchange system, which is found in all birds. The blood vessels, carrying warm blood down from their body, wrap around those coming back up, transferring heat to the cold blood flowing up from their feet. They can also control the rate of blood flow to their feet by varying the diameter of the blood vessels. It's a really efficient way of keeping their feet just a few degrees above freezing – warm enough to prevent frostbite without losing too much heat from their bodies.

To keep their feet from freezing, Emperor penguins hunch down so their bellies and feathers cover their legs.

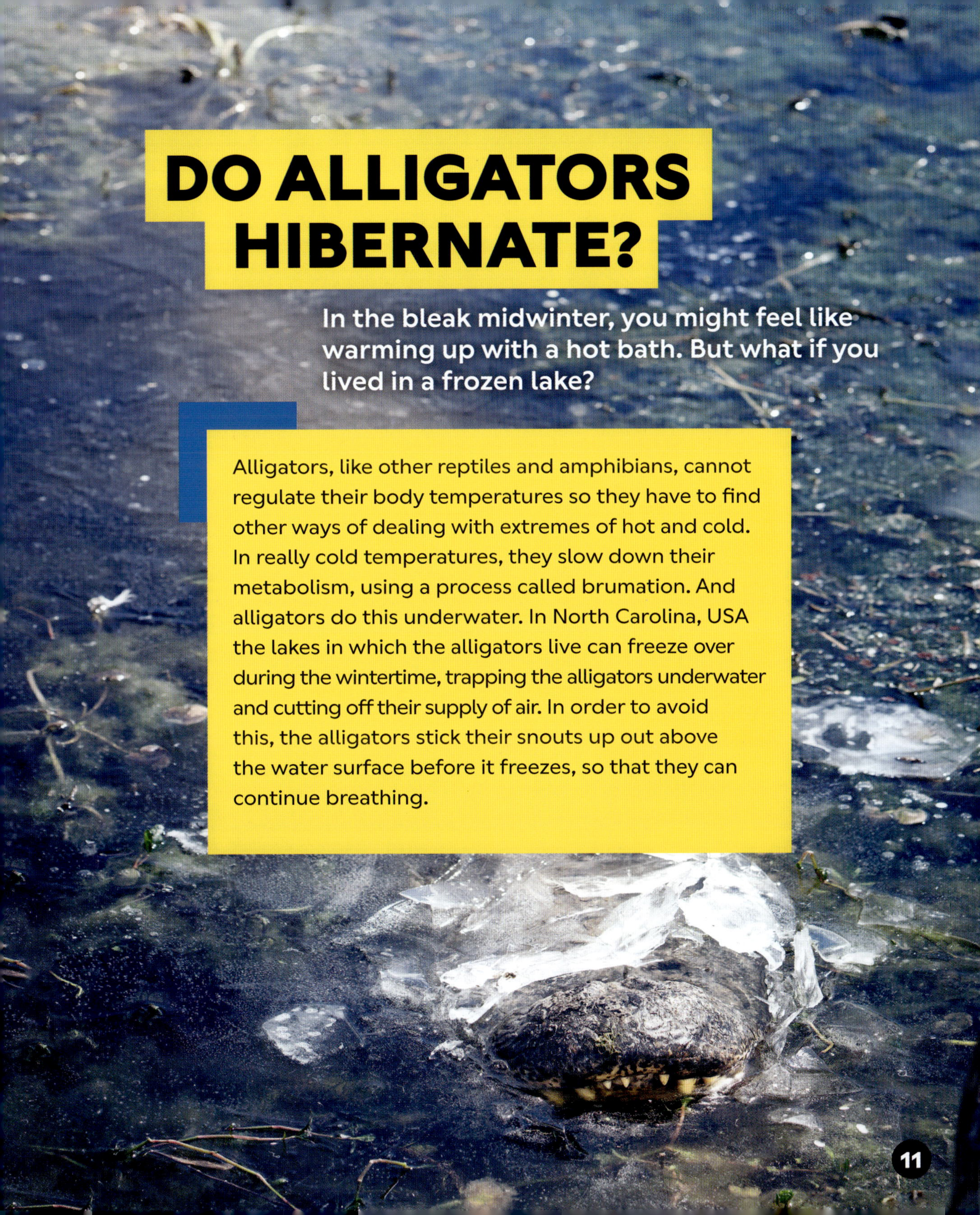

DO ALLIGATORS HIBERNATE?

In the bleak midwinter, you might feel like warming up with a hot bath. But what if you lived in a frozen lake?

Alligators, like other reptiles and amphibians, cannot regulate their body temperatures so they have to find other ways of dealing with extremes of hot and cold. In really cold temperatures, they slow down their metabolism, using a process called brumation. And alligators do this underwater. In North Carolina, USA the lakes in which the alligators live can freeze over during the wintertime, trapping the alligators underwater and cutting off their supply of air. In order to avoid this, the alligators stick their snouts up out above the water surface before it freezes, so that they can continue breathing.

WHY DO HONEYBEES DANCE?

Honeybees work together in a colony to gather food. When a female worker bee finds a good flower patch, it spreads the news by dancing.

The waggle dance is a fantastic means by which honeybees can communicate to their fellow workers exactly where a food source is relative to the hive. To do this they waggle their abdomens while they perform a little figure-of-eight dance. The number of circuits they do, and the intensity with which they vibrate their abdomens, relates to the quality of food. And the distance they cover relates to how far away the food is from the hive, while the angle that they move in is the angle of the food source relative to the sun. And the honeybees even compensate for the fact that the sun may have moved by the time they get back to the hive. The worker honeybees also communicate the smell to help identify the right nectar source. These are just a few of these fascinating insects' amazing behaviours.

WHY DO HYENAS LAUGH?

Spotted hyenas have a bad reputation. Historically they've been described as traitors or cowards, and their laugh can sound creepy. But the truth about these animals is quite the opposite.

Hyenas are actually very intelligent animals that live together in large social groups. Despite their reputation for being scavengers, they in fact hunt for most of their food and they're incredibly good at it, using all sorts of different kinds of communications to help them work together as a pack. One way in which they communicate is the funny noise that sounds to us like hysterical human laughter. In reality they generally make that sound when they feel threatened or are under attack. They make lots of other noises as well – whoops which can be heard over 5 km (3 miles) away, and grunts and yells. They also have different personality traits and are able to recognize each other and identify members of their own family.

WHY DO AYE-AYES DRUM ON TREES?

The aye-aye is a nocturnal primate from Madagascar. It taps on trees with its very long middle fingers. But why does it drum all night?

If the aye-aye hears something inside the tree trunk it gnaws a hole and then uses its middle finger to scoop out the prize.

Aye-ayes have a varied diet, but one thing they really like to eat is insect larvae. An aye-aye will tap on the bark of a tree at up to eight beats per second, using its big, funnel-shaped ears to listen for echoes which indicate a cavity under the bark likely to contain a tasty grub. Once it's found a likely spot, it uses its teeth to make a hole in the bark and fishes out the grub using its specially-evolved long, thin middle finger. This method of feeding is called percussive foraging. Another thing this funky creature uses its very long middle finger for is picking its nose! It inserts its 8 cm (3 in) long finger almost entirely into its nose, before pulling it out and licking it clean. Scientists are not sure why the aye-aye does this, but it is not alone in its nose-picking habits. Other primates (and not just humans) like chimpanzees, macaques and gorillas, have been observed picking their nose, and many others have been recorded using twigs to pick them as well.

A Tennessee fainting goat (left) goes stiff and a male goat (below left) lets out a loud bleating.

WHY DO GOATS SCREAM AND FAINT?

Some goats scream, others faint. What is really going on with goats?

Like human voices, goats have a variety of bleats which vary from goat to goat. Some sound like humans yelling or screaming, whereas others don't sound like us at all. Goats make noises for a range of reasons, such as when they're hurt or hungry, or trying to find members of their herd. Another bizarre behaviour amongst certain goats is fainting. This only happens to a particular breed of goat, the Tennessee fainting goat, and they don't really faint at all. They have a hereditary condition called myotonia congenita. When they are startled, they go a little bit stiff, which can sometimes mean that they fall over and look like they have fainted.

Eating your own poo might seem disgusting, but it's not a bad habit if you're a rabbit.

WHY DO RABBITS EAT THEIR OWN POO?

Rabbits are hindgut fermenters, which means that they digest their food in a single chamber of their stomach. Because of this, it's much harder for them to get all the nutrients that they need from their food. So, in order to get those nutrients, a rabbit passes its food through its digestive system twice, and to do this it produces two different types of poo. The first is caecotropes poo, which looks like dark, sticky pellets. It contains lots of minerals, proteins and nutrients that the rabbit needs. To extract these, the rabbit nibbles the poo and passes it through the digestive system again. It then produces a second type of poo, a faecal pellet that it doesn't eat.

Caecotropes poo (above) is full of nutrients, so rabbits nibble it up to get those nutrients, and then get rid of what is left by producing faecal pellets (top).

HAVE YOU EVER SEEN WORM POO AT THE BEACH?

Strange and curly, at low tide it's hard to miss. You might think all worm poos are the same. But below the surface there's a different story to be told.

Lugworms are very rarely seen but their casts reveal where their burrows are.

These are the worm casts, or poo, from small worms called lugworms, which live under the surface of the sand. At one end they swallow water and sand and then, at the other end, they excrete the sand, leaving little squiggles on the surface. Some lugworms produce a really neat, coiled spiral, while others produce a really messy squiggle. When research first started on these lugworms we thought that there was only one species. But in 1993 researchers discovered that there were actually two completely separate species of lugworm. And one of the easiest ways you can tell which is which, just from looking on the surface of the sand, is by checking whether the worm casts are squiggly or in a spiral.

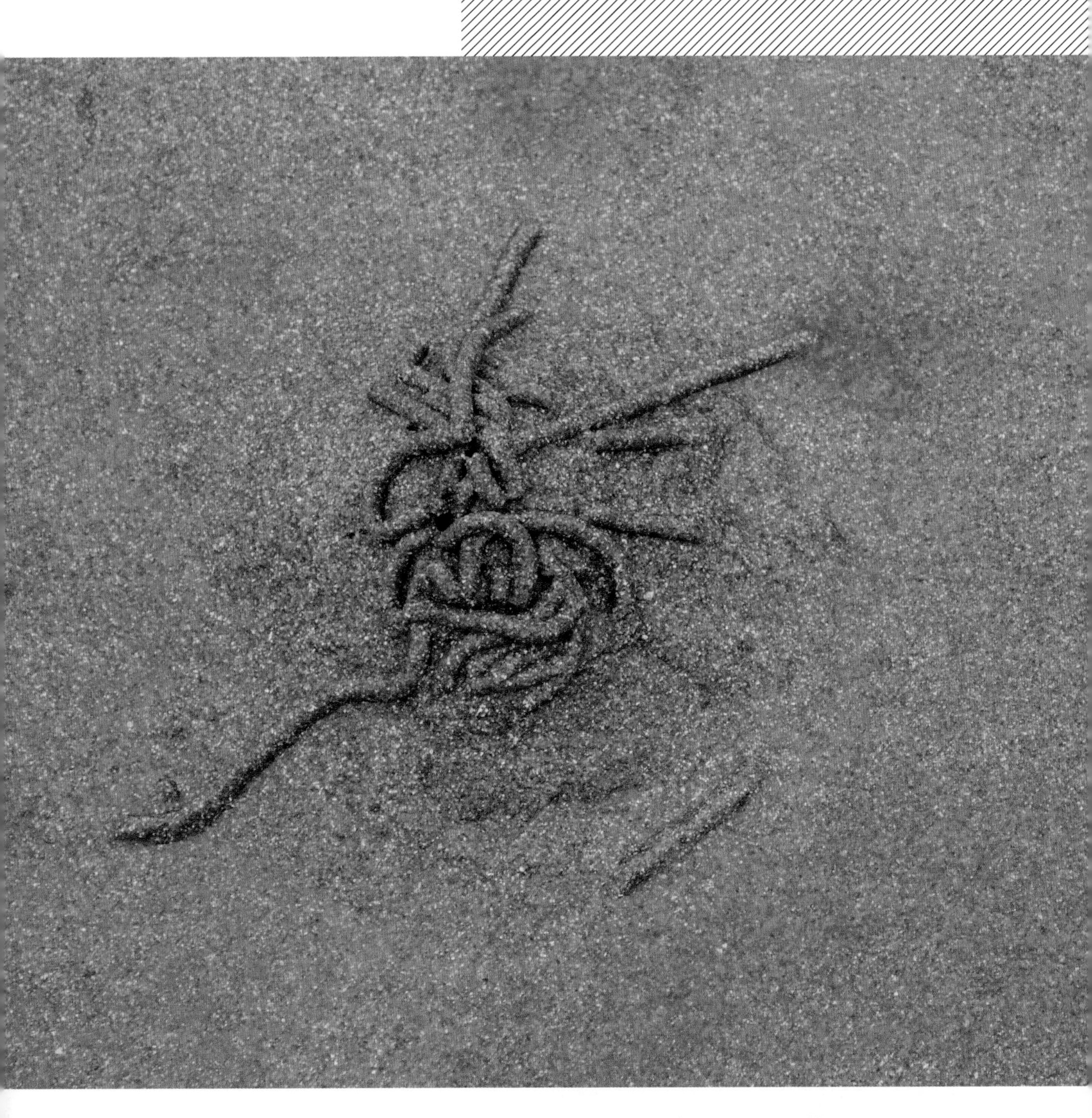

DO BIRDS POO OR PEE?

We've all seen the white splatters on cars, statues and windowsills, sometimes even our heads. But is it bird poo or pee that's falling from the sky?

Birds don't pee because they don't produce urine. Instead, they get rid of the excess nitrogen produced by their bodies in the form of uric acid, which is the white paste that we often see. However, many birds have another way of getting rid of food waste. They produce pellets or boluses, which are balls of bones, hair and other hard-to-digest bits of their dinners which they regurgitate. These are normally found at the base of the trees where the bird is nesting, especially in the case of owls. It might look like a ball of fur, but a pellet can tell us all about what the bird that has spit it out eats. So the next time a bird poo lands on your shoulder, be glad it's not a pellet of regurgitated prey!

A seagull (top) releasing white uric acid droppings mid flight. An owl pellet (above) – what the pellets look like depends on what the birds eat.

DO BIRDS SNEEZE?

Have you ever seen a penguin with a runny nose? Sometimes they even seem to sneeze. But it's not because they have a cold.

Seabirds eat fish and other seafood that they catch while swimming. Feeding in the ocean means swallowing a lot of saltwater and, to stop them from dehydrating, seabirds need a way to get rid of excess salt. So they have a gland right above their eyes called the supraorbital gland or salt gland. It filters salt from their bloodstream and they then excrete it through their nares, or nostrils, as a briny liquid. Often this salty fluid drips out and gives the appearance of a runny nose, and it can even discolour their feathers. But they also expel it by exhaling or shaking their heads; so it does look a bit like they're sneezing, but in fact they're just getting rid of a bit of salt.

The large nostril on this giant petrel's beak is clearly visible.

WHY DO SEALS HAVE WHISKERS?

Harbour and grey seals feed on fast-swimming fish such as herring, salmon and sand eels, using a secret weapon to track prey, even in murky waters.

Seals are able to detect fish because the fish, as they're swimming, leave a wake like a boat, a hydrodynamic trail that is detected by the seals' whiskers. The seals' whiskers are so sensitive that they can pick up those trails from over 100 m (330 ft) away, and they can do that while they're swimming. The seals' whiskers are not shaped like a straight drinking straw but are actually undulated. And it's that undulated structure that ensures that the whiskers hardly vibrate, even as the seal is swimming. And this allows them to be incredibly sensitive to detecting the trails left by the fish.

A harbour seal showcasing its incredible whiskers.

DO PLANTS EVER EAT MEAT?

The meat-eaters of the plant world are making a comeback - what could be more frightening!

This blow fly is stuck and is being eaten alive by the carnivorous sundew plant.

Carnivorous plants hold a grisly fascination for many people. They get the nutrients they need by attracting, trapping and digesting animals. There are currently around 630 species and most consume insects, but some of the larger ones are capable of digesting small reptiles and mammals, and aquatic species eat crustaceans and small fish. They use an assortment of traps and sticky tricks. Sundews for example, are a group of carnivorous plants that produce sticky, sweet-smelling fluid from little hairs on their leaves. When an insect lands on a leaf, the hairs curl around it and glue it into place. Eventually the whole leaf folds around the insect and special enzymes in the oozing fluid dissolve it. Carnivorous plants still need photosynthesis and root systems to survive - being carnivorous just helps the plants make the most of what's around them.

WHICH ANIMAL HAS SPINES IN ITS THROAT?

All sea turtles have beaks, but do they also have teeth?

Sea turtles have pointed prong-shaped protrusions in their throats called oesophageal papillae. These are sharp, backward-pointed spines that are not really teeth and are composed mostly of keratin. Sea turtles ingest a lot of water with their food, so the spines keep the jellyfish they eat in place, while the muscles of the oesophagus expel the excess water. Unfortunately plastic bags and plastic waste look a lot like their favourite prey item – jellyfish – and they end up ingesting the plastic waste and clogging up their intestines because the oesophageal papillae lining their throats make it very difficult for them to expel it.

A close up of the inside of a sea turtle's spike-coated throat.

DO VAMPIRE BATS REALLY SUCK BLOOD?

There are over 1,100 species of bat in the world though only three are known to feed on blood. Are they the evil bloodsuckers they are made out to be?

Firstly vampire bats don't actually suck blood. What they do is use heat sensors around their nose to detect areas where blood is near to the surface of the skin and cut through the skin with their very sharp teeth. They then lap up rather than suck up the blood that comes out, while an anticoagulant in their saliva ensures the blood continues to flow freely. There is also a somewhat softer side to vampire bats. Within a roost, if certain individuals haven't been able to feed, others sometimes share their blood meal with them. This may be because they hope that at some point in the future the gesture will be reciprocated. But that only works if everyone shares.

DOES AN EEL FEED DIFFERENTLY TO OTHER FISH?

Most fish feed using a method called suction feeding. They rapidly expand their mouth, suck in water, drawing their prey inside and down their throats. A moray eel can't do this.

Moray eels live in very narrow, confined, rocky spaces where there just isn't enough room to expand their heads and create the required suction. Also a lot of the prey they eat is too big and strong for this technique to work. So instead they have a set of movable jaws in the back of their throats. They attack their prey by biting with their front (oral) jaws. And then this second set of pharyngeal jaws is drawn forward, grabs the prey and then withdraws with the prey, taking it down into the eel's gullet. This set of pharyngeal jaws has terrifying, sharp, backwardly curved teeth all over it. Most bony fish have pharyngeal jaws and teeth, but only morays are known to move them forward in this manner.

WHAT GIVES JEWEL SCARABS THEIR GOLDEN GLOW?

There's a huge variety of beetle colours and jewel scarabs have some of the shiniest. But how do they get their glorious metallic gold colour?

Jewel scarabs come in a huge variety of colours, but probably the most well known are the metallic gold ones. You might think they get their colour through pigmentation, like our skin, but it's actually through what is known as structural colour. The surface of their shell is made up of tiny nanostructures that reflect the light in a way that polarizes it. The scarab beetle genus *Chrysina*, which is one of the only creatures that produces a metallic gold colour in the animal kingdom, is found in cloud forests in Central America, where they are probably mimicking

WHY DO CHAMELEONS CHANGE COLOUR?

For chameleons, changing colour is often more about standing out than blending in.

A green chameleon blending into its surroundings.

With their basic colours of green and brown, most chameleons already match their environment very well, and their ability to change colour is actually used much more for communication than camouflage. For example, when two rival males meet they try to establish dominance with a bright display of colour. Males also use colour to attract a mate and, if a female is not interested, she'll let the mate know by becoming darker. Chameleons can make these rapid colour changes because of special cells in their skin, called iridophores, which contain tiny reflective crystals. Stretching or compressing these iridophores changes the wavelength and therefore the colour of the light they reflect. This, combined with some pigments in their skin, produces the brilliant blues, reds and oranges we see in many chameleons.

When a panther chameleon feels threatened it changes colour and inflates its body.

WHY ARE FLAMINGOS PINK?

Baby flamingos aren't bright pink like their parent. So what causes their colourful transformation?

Flamingos get their bright colour from their diet and from what their diet eats. Flamingos are filter feeders, so they sweep through the mud and the water and take up everything they find, including algae, shrimps and insects. The shrimp, larvae and insects also eat algae. So algae, shrimps and larvae all have this orange colour that comes from a compound called carotenoid. This is the same compound that's also in pumpkins and carrots and gives them their orange colour. The flamingo digests its food and the orange-red colour gets absorbed into the feathers, turning them pink.

HOW DO BIRDS KEEP COOL?

Humans sweat to keep cool. Hippos wallow in mud. But birds have other ways to beat the heat.

The toco toucan (top) can change the amount of blood flow to and from its beak to prevent it from overheating, whereas other birds, such as the collared pratincole (above) pant to cool down.

Birds have a range of ways to stay cool. Some migrate or move up the mountains to find cooler climates. Some raise up their wings to increase air flow to their skin. And some birds, like toucans, can even change the blood flow through their beaks to get rid of excess heat – this is similar to how humans increase blood flow to their skin to regulate temperature. And, like dogs, birds can also pant, moving heat from inside their bodies to outside. This is more efficient than in mammals because birds have a one-way lung system. So while panting may seem strange to us, humans and birds both use water and air flow to regulate their temperatures.

HOW DO HIPPOS PROTECT THEMSELVES FROM THE SUN?

Hippos stay cool by spending time in water, but that doesn't protect them from damaging solar rays.

Hippos need to secrete a special substance to protect themselves from UV rays. It is often confused by humans with blood, but it's not. Rather it contains a red pigment called hipposudoric acid, which comes from the Latin for 'hippo' and 'sweat'. The substance also helps hippos keep their skin clear from harmful bacteria which is very important for them because they fight a lot with each other over territory and therefore often get cuts on their skin. Scientists are still working to understand how the substance is so effective. But, regardless, you don't want to cover yourself with this liquid if you've run out of sunscreen as it apparently smells awful.

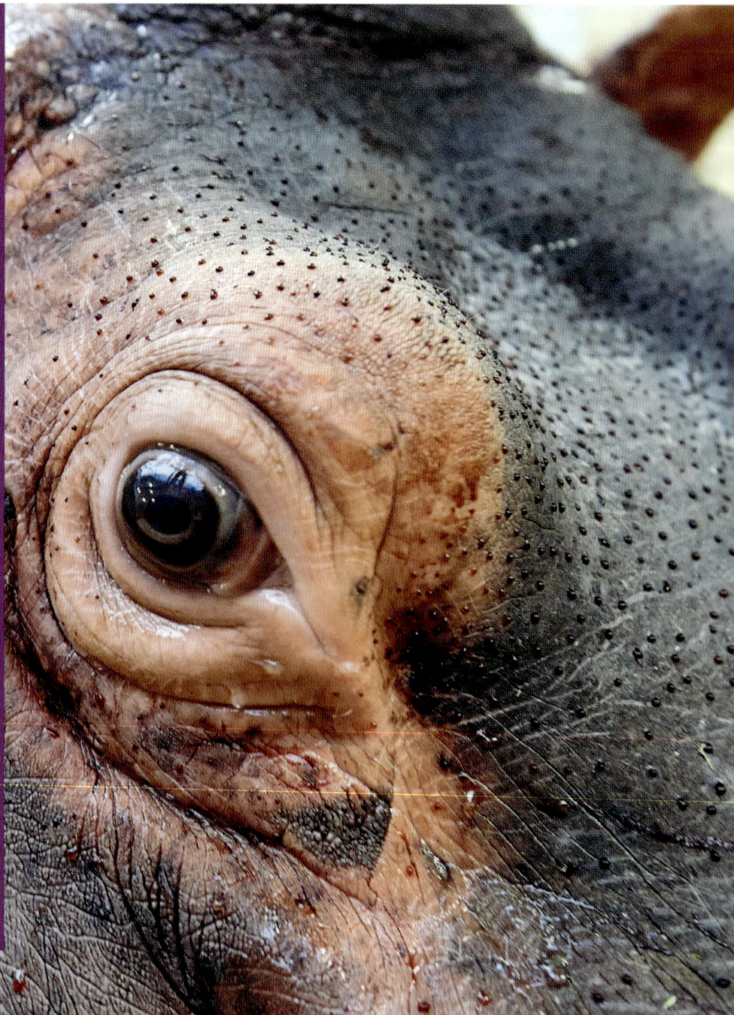

DO OCTOPUSES DREAM?

Octopuses need sleep just like us. But just how similar are their sleeping habits?

The white-spotted octopus sometimes changes colour while it sleeps – which could mean it dreams like we do.

By closely studying octopus and cuttlefish in the lab, scientists have been able to show that these cephalopods go through two phases of sleep – a slower phase and a more active phase. It's in the slow phase that they hardly move and their pupils are tightly closed. In the more active phase, their skin often changes colour and pattern. We humans go through similar phases. We go through a slower phase and then a faster, rapid REM phase of sleep. And it's during this REM phase of sleep that we dream. Whilst we don't know that octopuses dream like us in this active state, it's really interesting that two vastly different creatures undergo such similar stages of sleep patterns.

HOW DO BIRDS SLEEP?

Despite the images on social media, owls don't sleep lying down. But birds do have a surprising sleep adaptation.

A frigatebird can sleep on the wing, or in gliding flight. And a female eclectus parrot sleeps on a perch without falling off.

Birds can spend days, even weeks, in flight without stopping for a rest, travelling very long distances in search of food and warmth. They can do this because they have the ability to sleep while flying with, literally, one eye open. They do this by putting half their brain to sleep while keeping the other half awake, still aware of what's going on around them. This ability also allows them to sleep while perched on a branch, or while floating in water. And they're not the only animals that can do this. Dolphins and seals can also half-sleep while swimming. Many humans, would no doubt love to take half-naps too but, unfortunately, for us it's either all or nothing.

ARE AN OWL'S EARS REALLY EARS?

In some owls the ears, which you think are on the top or side of their heads, aren't really where you think they are.

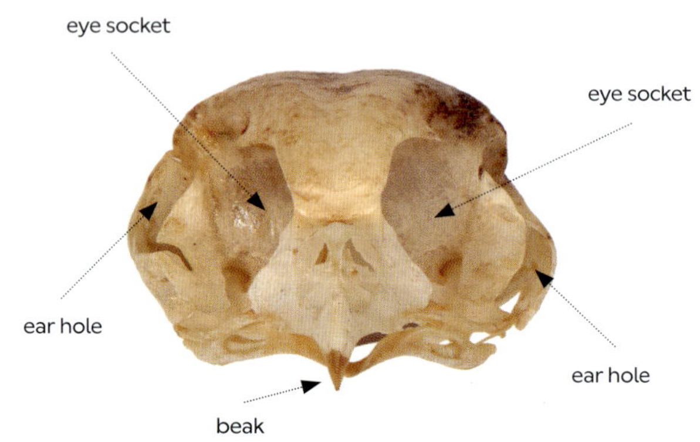

Rather than their ears being the tufts on the top of their heads, some owls have ears that are lower down and also asymmetrical - at different heights. When owls detect an interesting sound, they'll move their heads until that sound is received in both ears at exactly the same time. When that happens, the owl knows it's facing in the exact direction that the sound is coming from, and so it can find its prey. Owls don't have an external ear structure like many mammals, but they do have intricate feather designs that act as a satellite dish, focusing the sounds into their ears.

The most asymmetric owl skulls are those of *Aegolius* species – like this northern saw-whet owl, *Aegolius acadicus* – and *Strix nebulosa* and *S. uralensis,* though these don't have ear tufts.

HOW MANY OWLS IN AN OWL CALL?

Have you ever heard the call of a tawny owl? Even if you're not aware that what you're hearing is a tawny owl, people tend to be familiar with the 'too-wit too-woo' sound of this animal.

What people might not know is that this call is done by not one, but two birds. The duet has two parts. The 'too-wit' or 'kewick' sound is made by the female and is a contact call. The owl does this to let other owls know that it's around. After this you usually hear the second part of the call. This 'too-woo', or more exactly 'hoohoo' is made by the male responding to the female and is also to let other males know that this is its turf. This is a territorial call. So, if you hear the 'too-wit too-woo' of a tawny owl, you know that you have not one, but two visitors to your neighbourhood.

HOW CLEVER IS AN OCTOPUS?

Octopuses are some of the most intelligent animals on Earth. They can open jars, use tools and play with objects. But not all of their neurons are found in one brain.

In humans and other vertebrates the nervous system is centralized into the brain and the neurons that run around the body. In octopuses, around two thirds of the neurons are actually found in their arms and these are localized into small brains called ganglia. These ganglia are involved in touch, used for sensing chemicals, and it's even thought that they could be used to sense light as well. Because of this localized control they can be used for things like catching food, escaping from predators, manipulating objects and sensing the environment around them.

CAN JELLYFISH LIVE FOREVER?

Is it possible to live forever? While most organisms grow old over time there is one animal that can stay forever young.

The tiny jellyfish *Turritopsis dohrnii* is one of the few known animals that can be considered truly immortal! It has the unusual ability to revert to a younger stage of its life after it reaches maturity. Jellyfish normally go through a life cycle that begins with an egg that slowly grows to a larva. This attaches to a rock or another solid surface where it continues to grow, becoming a polyp. Once the polyp is big enough, it starts to bud off and the adult jellyfish (known as a medusa) drifts into the ocean. In the case of the immortal jellyfish, after it reaches its mature adult stage it can revert back to the polyp stage before growing into an adult once again. Potentially this can be repeated indefinitely, resulting in a jellyfish that won't die of old age - a true immortal organism! Many of them do die however, since they can still catch disease or be preyed upon by predators. But in perfect conditions they could theoretically live forever.

WHY DOES RAIN SMELL?

Who doesn't enjoy the smell of rain? The source of this scent may surprise you.

The unique and familiar smell of rain is caused by raindrops hitting the dry ground and releasing different natural compounds into the air. This scent is called petrichor. It is made of oils produced by plants and a molecule called geosmin. Geosmin is a compound produced by certain bacteria and microscopic algae called cyanobacteria, the main reason behind the smell of rain. Don't worry, it is not toxic to humans, but our noses are really, really sensitive to it and we can smell it in really tiny concentrations when it's in the air. This explains why we are able to smell it everywhere when it rains, even if we are in the middle of the city with concrete pavements and without much open soil.

CAN ANIMALS REALLY BE FRIENDS?

In nature, different species sometimes work together, helping each other to thrive. This is called mutualism and can lead to some surprising relationships.

One example of mutualism is between the hornbill and the dwarf mongoose. When the dwarf mongoose pack goes out hunting, the hornbill follows them and catches any insects that they disturb. In return the hornbill warns the mongoose if any predators are approaching, by calling really loudly. The mongooses wait for the hornbills before they go out hunting in the morning and, if the mongooses have slept in late, the hornbill will sometimes wake them up by calling or tapping outside of their den.

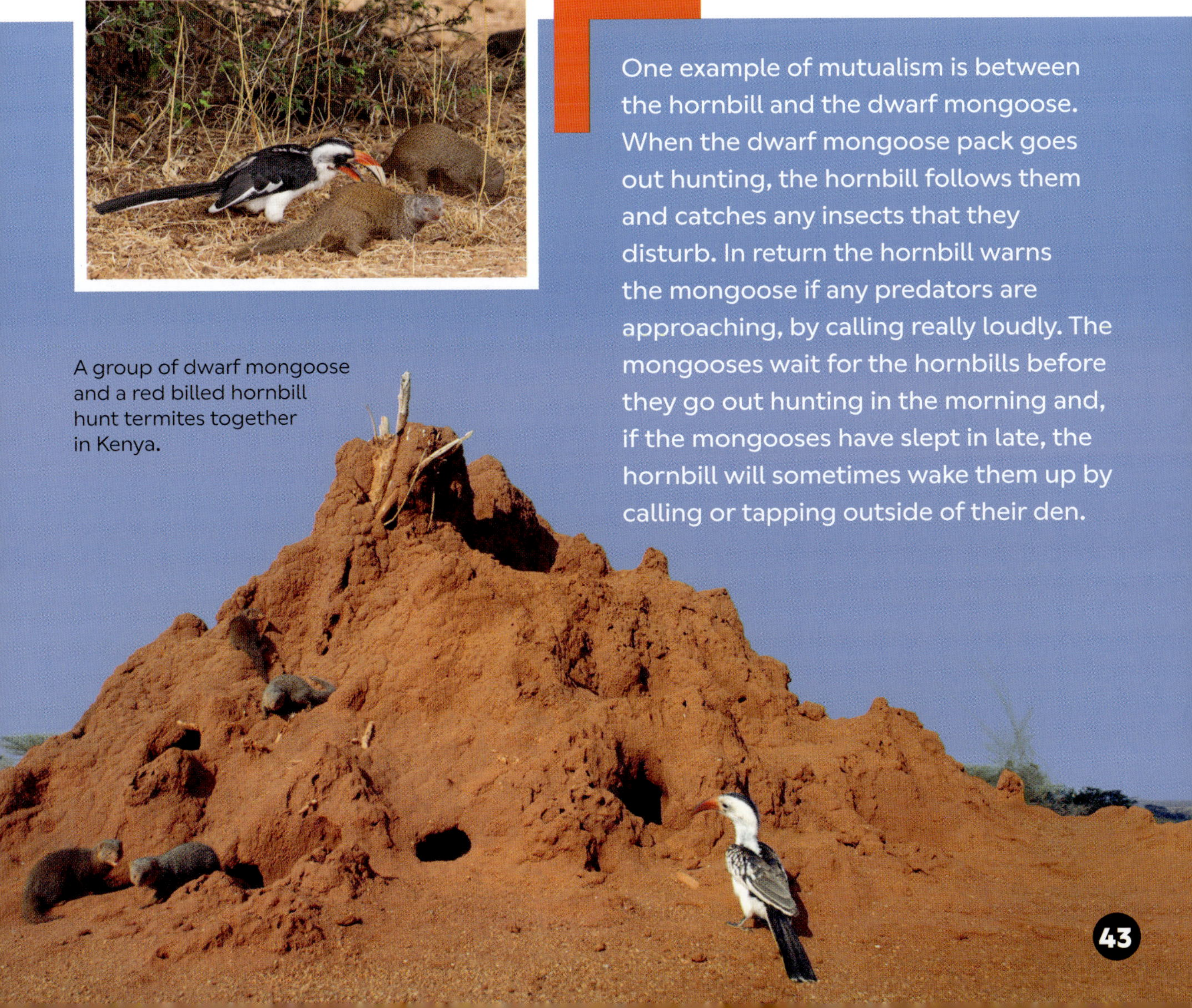

A group of dwarf mongoose and a red billed hornbill hunt termites together in Kenya.

WHAT IS ANTARCTICA'S BIGGEST ANIMAL?

Antarctica's biggest land animal is smaller than you might think. But it's a tough customer.

The largest land animal in Antarctica is a small midge about 2-6 mm long, called *Belgica antarctica*. It spends most of its two-year life cycle as a larva in the soil, where temperatures only drop to about -5°C (23°F), even though it might be -40°C (-40°F) above ground. The larvae also produce chemicals that act as antifreeze, so it can go down to -7°C (19°F) before ice forms within its body. If temperatures do go lower than that, the larvae can tolerate some freezing and they produce special heat shock proteins that repair cell damage caused by the freezing. The adults also produce antifreeze chemicals, but they only live for about 10 days during the year, so are less likely to come across these cold conditions. So this might be quite a tiny insect, but it's a pretty tough one given its environment.

WHAT POLLINATES CHOCOLATE?

Bees are championed as superstar pollinators, but who are the other extremely important pollinators who have been successfully helping plants reproduce for over 200 million years?

Pictured is the fruit of the cocoa tree, *Theobroma cacao*, which literally translates as 'cacao, food of the gods', and it's from this that we get chocolate. That we do is largely thanks to the tiny little fly pictured above, the midge *Forcipomyia*. And it's not just cocoa that's pollinated by midges. More than 100 cultivated crops are pollinated by a diverse range of flies. These include mangoes, apples, pears, cherries, strawberries, plums, apricots, peaches, raspberries, blackberries, bell peppers, cayenne peppers, black pepper, coriander, jalapenos, carrots, onions, parsley and more.

WHAT USES LIGHT AS DISGUISE?

Lanternfishes may be small, but they make up over half the total mass of fish in the deep sea. Every night, they move as a huge group from the deep to the ocean's surface. This is one of the largest movements of animals on the planet.

There are nearly 250 species of lanternfishes and some of them look very similar. Fortunately each species has a characteristic pattern of light organs, called photophores, along the sides of their body and belly, and we can use these to identify the different species. We've still a lot to learn about lanternfishes, including the function of those photophores. We think these little blue-green lights, when viewed from below, balance the light coming from the surface of the ocean so that the outline of the fish is broken up and the silhouette is harder for predators to see – this is called counter-illumination.

DOES ANYTHING LIVE AT THE BOTTOM OF THE OCEAN?

In the deep ocean, hydrothermal vents spew toxic chemicals and minerals into the water. Remarkably, life thrives here in a multitude of shapes and forms, including these giant 2 m (6½ ft) tubes.

These tube worms don't have a mouth, gut or anus but are still able to feed themselves. And they play a really important role within hydrothermal vent ecosystems. The worm uses its flashy, red, feathery top to absorb certain chemicals that come out of the vents. It then transfers these to vast colonies of bacteria living inside its body. The bacteria use these compounds to create nutrients for the giant tube worms that they inhabit, and these nutrients are also available for other inhabitants of the vents.

The red, feathery tops of the tube worms absorb chemicals spewed out of the vents. Bacteria in the worms use these to make nutrients for the worms.

WHAT HAS ITS HOME INSIDE A FISH'S MOUTH?

Sea anemones provide a home for colourful clownfish. But clownfish also shelter their own inhabitants.

The eyes peering out of the clownfish's mouth belong to a parasitic isopod. The isopod attaches itself to the tongue of the clownfish with its hook-like legs, called pereopods, and the tongue begins to degenerate. When the isopod matures you often see a pair of male and female isopods inside the mouth cavity, with the female being the larger one. They reproduce in the mouth cavity, and the female rear the young in a marsupium, or pouch, on the underside of their body. These young are then released into the water as free-living juveniles. The presence of the isopod can also eventually affect the size the fish grows to.

WHAT'S WEIRD ABOUT ANGLERFISH?

There are many things that are weird about anglerfish, but possibly the weirdest thing of all is that in one group of anglerfish the female is six times bigger than the male.

Ceratiidae is a group of anglerfishes known as seadevils. They are found in the ocean at depths of 200 m (656 ft) to 4,000 m (13,123 ft), where it is pitch-black. Females can grow up to 1 m (3 ft) long – the largest known species is *Ceratias holboelli* – and, in contrast, the male reaches a maximum size of about 15 cm (6 in). The male has massive nostrils and, using these, is able to smell the female in the dark and attach to her body. His mouthparts recede and merge into the female, and their blood systems fuse. So, the male becomes like a parasite – he has a permanent supply of food for the rest of his life, and she has a permanent supply of sperm. It's quite a bizarre relationship but it works perfectly.

WHAT ANIMAL HEADBUTTS TO DEFEND ITSELF?

There are many different kinds of poison dart frogs, their different colours advertising how toxic they are. These colourful creatures have been carefully studied, but a recent discovery about frogs that use their toxins as venom has come as a surprise.

Venom is physically injected into a target, like a snake does with its fangs. But most frogs don't have a way of injecting venom so they protect themselves by being poisonous instead. Greening's frog however is one of two species that we now know inject venom, using spines protruding from its head. When it is attacked by a would-be predator the frog headbutts its assailant. Tiny bones in its upper lip thrust out of its skin, pass through venom glands, picking up venom, and then deliver it into a would-be predator. This can cause extreme pain and possible death, so we think it's a pretty effective defence.

WHAT DISGUISES ITSELF AS A SNAKE?

Moths spend most of their lives as caterpillars. At this stage they are vulnerable to predators so, to deter them, they have evolved strategies such as warning colourations and camouflage. But some species have taken things a step further.

Hemeroplanes triptolemus is a type of hawkmoth found throughout Central and South America. The caterpillar of this hawkmoth has an incredible defence strategy. By retracting its legs and inflating its front body segment, it resembles the head of a snake, complete with scales and eye-like spots. The caterpillar does a great job of mimicking snake behaviour too, even to the point where it strikes at potential predators. This amazing disguise can startle and intimidate birds and other potential predators, and it can fool humans too.

WHAT INSECT DEFENDS ITSELF WITH BOILING, SMELLY LIQUID?

From spikes, to camouflage, to detachable tails, there is a huge range of different ways in which animals protect themselves. But one type of beetle takes it to the next level and packs a boiling explosive punch!

One of over 500 types of bombardier beetle. Their name comes from the chemical 'bombs' they can release.

There are around 400,000 species of beetle, and one group, the bombardier beetle, has one of the most extraordinary defence strategies of any animal. They are small beetles that live in the leaf litter and under stones and may be attacked by animals such as toads and shrews. In their abdomens, they have two chambers, each with different chemicals. One has hydroquinone and the other has hydrogen peroxide. When these chemicals are separate, they are harmless, but when the beetle is threatened by a predator, it mixes them together in a chamber at the end of the thorax. When they mix, the reaction creates heat of nearly 100°C (212°F) and turns the fluid into vapour. The pressure this creates then actually fires the mixture out of a valve at the end of the beetle's thorax! Any predators get a faceful of a boiling, and horrible smelling liquid, and the beetle can scuttle out of harm's way.

A bombardier beetle releasing a rapid burst of stinky, burning-hot liquid from its rear end.

WHAT WINS THE PRIZE OF DISGUISE?

Some moths and butterflies are masters of disguise. They showcase a remarkable ability to blend into their environment and fool potential predators.

Flashes of luminous colour on the upper side of the Indian leaf butterfly are revealed when it is in flight.

Moths and butterflies fall prey to a wide diversity of predators, so their ability to survive and reproduce depends on them remaining hidden in their environment. The classic example is the Indian leaf butterfly, also know as the dead leaf butterfly. Its upper side has shining orange and blue colours, but the underside has a striking resemblance to a dead leaf. An extraordinary example among moths is the Oriental prominent moth, *Uropyia meticulodina*. Many predators would be challenged to spot it nestling among the leaves on a branch or in the leaf litter. Its wing scales create the three-dimensional effect of a dried leaf that curls in on itself. This optical illusion is so effective that even a moth specialist would find it impossible to spot. These are two examples of the very rare three-dimensional patterns in the wings of butterflies and moths.

The oriental prominent moth, *Uropyia meticulodina*, (opposite) looks like a curled dried leaf on the forest floor.

WHAT CLEVER DEFENCES DO OCTOPUSES USE TO SURVIVE?

The open ocean is a hazardous place if you are the size of a grape. But one tiny octopus is armed and dangerous.

Tiny male blanket octopuses have developed an astonishing way of defending themselves. They are immune to the stings of the tentacles of the Portuguese man o' war, and so they move into the creature's mass of tentacles, rip some of them off and use them like whips. The females, which are much bigger, have a completely different defence strategy. They have webbing between their first and second arms, which they can unfurl to make themselves look big and scary. It's a brilliant way to keep predators at arm's length! The blanket octopus also exhibits the most extreme sexual dimorphism of all known animals existing on Earth today. The females grow to nearly 2 m (6 ft) while the males grow to only about 2½ cm (1 in).

The huge female blanket octopus with unfurled 'wings' (left) and the much much smaller male (above), which defends itself with tentacles ripped off from the Portuguese man-of-war.

WHICH ANIMAL IS THE KING OF MIGRATION?

During September to early November, millions of monarch butterflies migrate from Canada to Mexico, some flying as high as 3 km (2 miles) and as far as 5,000 km (3,100 miles). In March they journey back north. But no individual butterfly completes the entire round trip.

At least four generations are involved in the monarch's annual life cycle. During the northern migration, females lay eggs, which produce the next generation. The first three generations of monarchs complete their life cycle in just five to seven weeks. But when September comes again, a special fourth generation of monarch butterflies is produced – so called super monarchs. These make use of air currents to fly all the way to Mexico, and they live four to five times longer than their northwards-migrating ancestors. Monarchs follow the same routes that their ancestors took, sometimes even returning to the exact same tree as their great-great grandparents.

Large groups of monarch butterflies gather on trees in their wintering grounds in Mexico.

DO ALL FLIES HAVE WINGS?

Believe it or not this isn't a spider. You just need to count its legs to realize that this little creature is two legs shy of a spider. It's actually a fly, but without wings!

A wingless bat fly clings tightly with its amazing, hooked claws to the face of a Mozambican long-fingered bat.

This creature is one of the wingless bat flies. These flies are ectoparasites on bats and they're adapted to spend most of their lives clinging to their bat host. Many of the species have lost their wings and their flight muscles have been reduced to nothing. As a result, they've lost the ability to fly but their legs have developed strong muscles, bristles and claws so they can hold on tightly to the bat's fur and skin. And if you thought that was bizarre, these flies don't lay eggs – they give birth to live young! Not only that, the mothers only have one baby at a time, feeding it with a milky substance from lactating glands within her body.

A yellowhammer in the UK (above) and New Zealand (below) have different songs even though they are the same species.

Birdsong is one of the most instantly recognisable sounds in nature. The cacophony of sound that we hear at dawn tells us that the birds are awake and ready for the day. To the untrained ear it can sound like just a whole bunch of high-pitched sounds, but each species has its own unique call and, if you listen really carefully, you'll start to notice subtle differences within each species. Evidence suggests that birds have regional dialects. For example, town birds have a slightly higher pitch than birds from the countryside. And in the case of the yellowhammer, those living in New Zealand have a completely different song from those in the UK, even though genetically they're the same bird.

DO BIRDS HAVE LOCAL DIALECTS?

Would a pigeon in London sound the same as a pigeon in New York, or Sydney? Humans have a wide variety of dialects but what about birds?

CAN DOLPHINS TALK TO EACH OTHER?

In the 1960s, scientists tried to teach English to a bottlenose dolphin. It didn't work. But dolphins can, in a way, learn new ways of communication.

Killer whales (which are a type of dolphin) and bottlenose dolphins (top) communicate using sound within their groups. They can also change their communication sounds within their group so that the other groups can't understand them.

We know that dolphins communicate in complex ways with members of their own species, and they do this by combining clicks, whistles and pulses. Not only this but, in one study, scientists realized that captive killer whales, which are the largest dolphins, were copying the communication sounds of the bottlenose dolphins that they were housed with. And it seems that the killer whales were adapting their communication sounds so that they could socialize better. Things are very different in the wild, though. There's evidence that bottlenose dolphins alter their communication sounds so that they won't be heard or hunted by killer whales. So, it seems that dolphins are perfectly capable of learning new ways to communicate for themselves and they don't need our help to do it.

WILL AN ASTEROID HIT EARTH?

Asteroids were created when our solar system formed 4.6 billion years ago. Today there are around 800,000 asteroids orbiting the sun, and a few are potentially hazardous to Earth. Just how difficult is it to predict their movements?

Just like the Earth, asteroids rotate as they orbit the sun. When one side is facing the sun, the surface heats up and absorbs that heat. As it rotates away from the sun, the surface cools and radiates that heat outwards. This gives the asteroid a small kick in the opposite direction. This is known as the Yarkovsky effect. The effect is tiny, but because asteroids have spent billions of years in the solar system, it can add up to notable changes. Although we can't perfectly predict the orbits of asteroids, and whether one will impact the Earth at some point in the future, it's incredibly unlikely and not worth losing sleep over just yet.

It can happen that the moon actually appears a different colour than normal. The moonlight we see is reflected white light from the sun. And if there's something in the way that blocks the red light, the moon can appear blue. That can sometimes happen after volcanic eruptions. For example, after Krakatoa erupted in 1883 the moon was blue for over a year. The ash from the volcano was just the right size to block the red light and the moon appeared blue. We even know instances where the sun can appear blue due to particles from forest fires or volcanoes on Earth.

WHAT IS A BLUE MOON?

'Once in a blue moon' is a popular phrase, meaning very rarely. But where on earth did it come from?

WHAT ARE THE DARK SPOTS ON THE MOON?

The moon is a massive 383,000 km (23,8000 miles) from Earth, but some features on its surface can be seen with the naked eye. Mysterious dark patches called 'lunar maria', Latin for 'moon seas', are visible. Early astronomers saw these dark patches and thought they were oceans on the moon. Were they right or were they wrong?

The lunar maria aren't seas as we would understand them because they aren't made of water. But, there were once seas of molten lava. In the early solar system there were a lot of impacts, and many of these were into the young moon. Some of these triggered volcanism, which created huge pools of molten rock on the surface of the moon, which then solidified to form a rock called basalt – these are the dark splodges that we can see on the moon today. It may seem ridiculous that people once thought that there were actually seas on the moon, but they were almost correct in that there were seas there – it's just they were made of molten rock instead of water.

The near side of the moon always faces towards Earth and has bright highlands and dark seas of solidified lava.

HOW DO LAND SNAILS MATE?

Cupid's arrow takes on a whole new meaning for snails. Most land snails are hermaphrodites, meaning they have both male and female genitalia. Mating involves an elaborate courtship dance usually ending in an exchange of sperm, and some groups of land snails also fire 'love darts' into their partner's body.

Most land snails are promiscuous, mating with multiple partners. They either use the sperm they receive to fertilize their eggs, or they store the sperm and digest it. Love darts are a way of transferring hormones from one snail to another. These hormones stop the recipient from digesting the sperm and guide more of the sperm to the eggs where they are fertilized. This is great for the darter but not for the snail being darted. Studies have shown that darted snails have fewer offspring and have shorter lives.

HOW DOES A BEDBUG MATE?

Animals mate in all sorts of ways, some ways more surprising than others. And this is certainly the case with bedbugs.

The dagger-shaped penis of the male bed bug pierces through the female's body, then sperm is injected.

The male bedbug's penis is quite extraordinary. It is shaped a bit like a dagger and the male bedbug uses it to pierce through the female's body, generally through the abdomen, and inject its sperm. The sperm then has to travel to the female's ovaries, where it fertilizes the awaiting eggs and the offspring are born. Bedbugs aren't the only animals to practice what we call traumatic insemination. We see this in lots of other insects and creatures such as worms and sea slugs.

WHY SHOULD MALE SPIDERS BE WARY OF FEMALE SPIDERS?

Spider mating is a hazardous affair. Choosing the wrong partner can be deadly. The larger female may decide to eat her smaller mate.

Male peacock spiders, from the jumping spider family, flash and wiggle the colourful flaps on their abdomen to attract females, who then decide whether they will mate with or try to eat the male.

Male spiders have evolved different behaviours to encourage mating. The tiny male golden orb-weaver gives its much larger mate a back rub to calm her and make her more receptive to him, and less likely to eat him! Male nursery web spiders wrap up prey items in silk parcels, which they present to the female as a gift. While she unwraps and eats her present, he can mate with her. But an extraordinary behaviour is used by jumping spiders. These tiny arachnids perform elaborate dances to impress potential partners. This dance allows the male to identify himself to the female from a safe distance, without fear of being eaten.

Worms engage in courtship by visiting one another's burrows, often more than once before finally selecting a mate. It's thought they choose their mate based on the quality of their burrow. Earthworms are simultaneous hermaphrodites, which means they have both male and female reproductive organs. During mating, both sets of sex organs are used. If all goes well each earthworm becomes a genetic mother of some of its offspring and the genetic father of the rest. Many earthworm species can reproduce throughout the year. It's a very efficient way of making more earthworms.

HOW DO WORMS REPRODUCE?

Finding a partner isn't easy, even for the humble earthworm. Mating in the earthworm world is more complex than you might think.

During mating, two worms line up in the opposite position from each other so they can both give and receive sperm.

ARE ALL ANIMAL SCREAMS AS TERRIFYING AS THEY SOUND?

Ever heard an unearthly scream in the dead of night? The blood-curdling calls of animals are a feature of winter nights and may explain where many of our ghost stories come from.

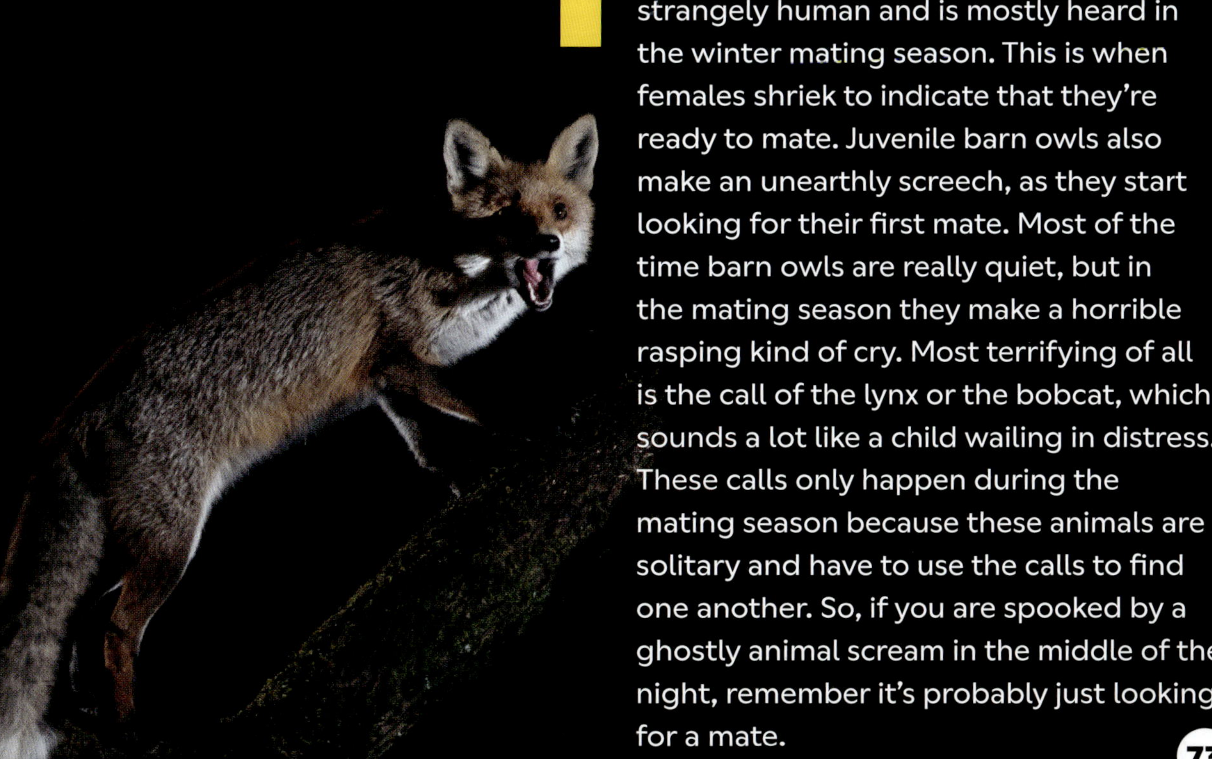

The scream of the red fox can seem strangely human and is mostly heard in the winter mating season. This is when females shriek to indicate that they're ready to mate. Juvenile barn owls also make an unearthly screech, as they start looking for their first mate. Most of the time barn owls are really quiet, but in the mating season they make a horrible rasping kind of cry. Most terrifying of all is the call of the lynx or the bobcat, which sounds a lot like a child wailing in distress. These calls only happen during the mating season because these animals are solitary and have to use the calls to find one another. So, if you are spooked by a ghostly animal scream in the middle of the night, remember it's probably just looking for a mate.

WHY DOES THIS MOTH GIVE GIFTS?

Gift giving is not a uniquely human trait. There are many examples in nature.

The six-spot burnet moth is a striking, day-flying moth, with a black metallic body, six vibrant red spots on each of its forewings and bright red hindwings. Its conspicuous look serves as a warning to would-be predators that it is loaded with toxic cyanide and is not likely to taste very nice. This powerful chemical is crucial for these moths because it also makes a delightful gift – if you are a female six-spot burnet moth! During mating, the male moth transfers a gift of cyanide to the female. It seems that this nuptial gift could boost the chance of the father's offspring surviving, since the mother can use the cyanide gift to increase protection for the eggs and the developing caterpillars.

WAS RUDOLPH A MALE OR FEMALE REINDEER?

Rudolph, one of Santa Claus's reindeer, was a female. We know this because during the wintertime Rudolph sports beautiful antlers.

In most deer species, antlers can help us tell male and female deer apart. Generally, males have antlers and females don't. But reindeer are an exception. Female reindeers do have antlers and, while males shed theirs in early December (winter in the northern hemisphere) after the mating season, females keep theirs. In the cold, snowy environments where they live, females, who are normally pregnant at this time, keep their antlers to protect themselves against predators and only shed them after giving birth. They need to defend their territory and any food they may have found, in order to survive and give birth to a healthy fawn. So, when you see Rudolph depicted with antlers, you now know this means that Rudolph was female.

DO SHARKS LAY EGGS?

Eggs are used by many animal species to protect and feed their young as they develop. Most have the same classic shape. But what animal could possibly have an spiral ridged egg like this?

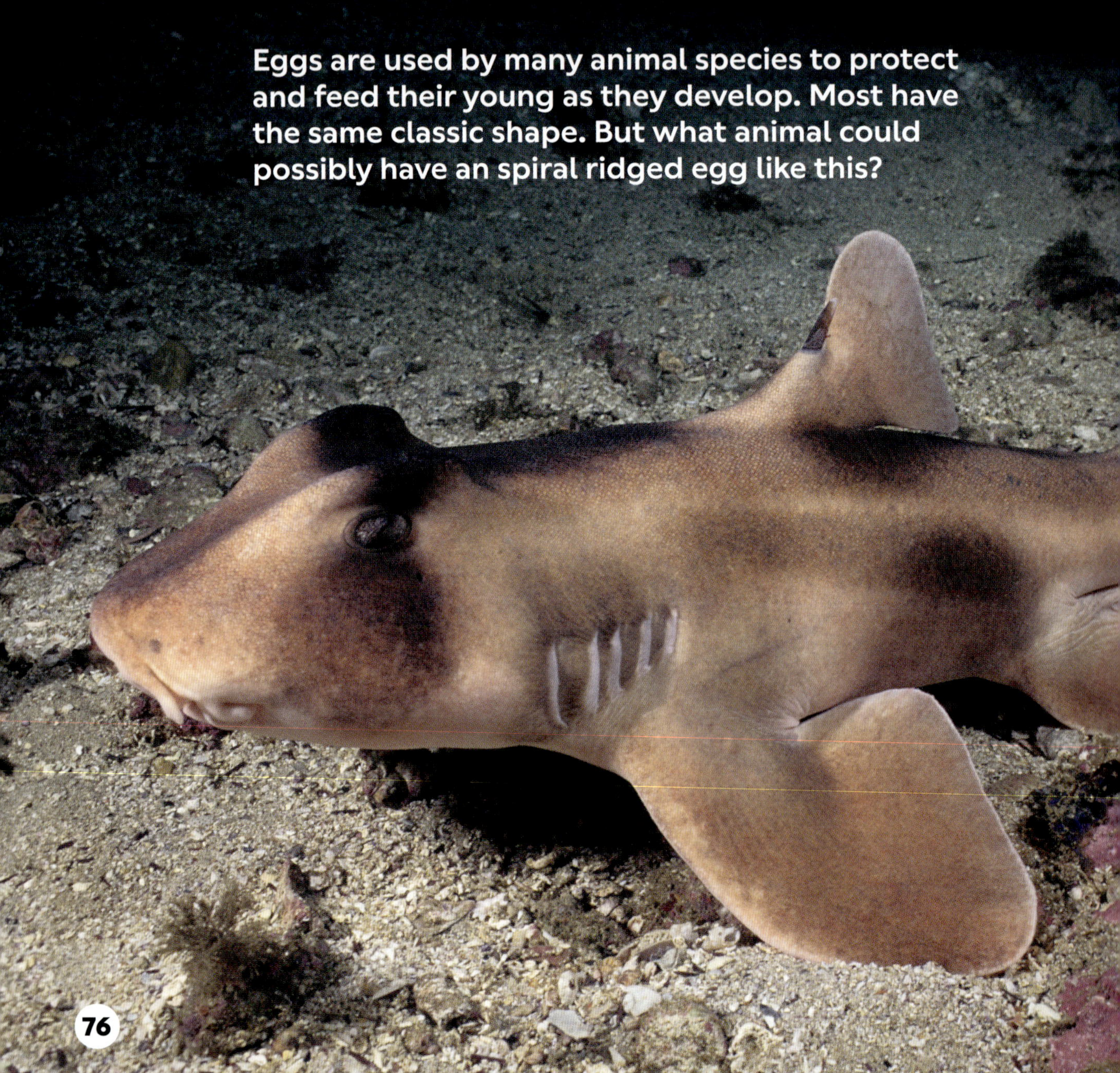

The spiral ridges of the bullhead shark's egg case hold the egg in rocky nooks and crannies so the currents don't sweep it away.

When you first look at this egg, it doesn't look like an egg at all, but it is - it is the egg of a bullhead shark. These eggs are specifically adapted to cope with being laid in the sea. When the female shark lays its egg, it carries it around in its mouth until it finds a suitable gap in the rocks. Once it finds the gap it places the egg inside it and the corkscrew-like shape of the egg helps hold it in place, so the ocean current doesn't wash it away. Each egg contains an embryo and a yolk sac which the embryo feeds off, helping it to develop inside the egg. Sharks have had eggs in this way for hundreds of millions of years and you can find these in the fossil record. So, whilst these might not be the classic egg shape, these bullhead shark eggs are perfectly adapted to their environment.

HOW DOES WEATHER AFFECT THE SEX OF SEA TURTLES?

Turtles spend their lives at sea. But they come ashore to lay eggs. The weather can have a surprising effect on them.

A hatchling loggerhead sea turtle emerges from its underground nest on a sandy beach in Australia.

Sea turtle eggs are laid in clutches in the sand on beaches. The temperature of the sand and surrounding environment affects the sex of the turtle that hatches – a warmer environment leads to females, while a cooler one leads to more males. This phenomenon is widespread in many ancient reptiles such as turtles, crocodiles and some lizards and is called temperature-dependent sex determination. A difference of only a few degrees can change the sex of an entire clutch of eggs. Global warming is putting the future of many turtle species at risk. As the world heats up, fewer males and more females are being born. When the females reach maturity they may struggle to find a mate and species could very quickly see their populations crash. Turtles have survived climate change before but the current speed of change may prove too much for them.

Like many marine turtle species, loggerhead sea turtle females will travel thousands of miles to return to the beach they hatched on to lay their own eggs.

WHY AREN'T SOME EGGS 'EGG-SHAPED'?

Eggs come in all shapes and sizes, and some are stranger shapes than others.

Guillemots colonies are so tightly packed that their territories extend only to a beak's-length around their chosen spot.

Guillemot eggs are some of the most extraordinary in the bird world. They come in a variety of colours and patterns and have an unusual pyriform or pear shape. Guillemots breed on narrow cliff ledges, and don't build nests. Their colonies are crowded, messy places. Each female lays a similarly patterned and coloured egg throughout her life, but different females can lay very different eggs. This infinite variation may allow the females to recognize and thus incubate their own eggs amongst all the others. Recent research suggests this shape may have evolved as it is inherently more stable on a slope. It may also give greater strength to the shell and so give it more protection.

HOW DO CAMELS SURVIVE IN DESERTS?

Can you picture a camel in the snow? Camels are adapted to live in deserts. But we tend to forget that deserts can be hot and cold.

Arabian or dromedary camels have a single hump (left) and Bactrian camels have two humps (below). Remarkably camels can survive months without drinking any water.

Camels can live in extreme environments, from boiling hot to freezing cold ones. Their humps are a great adaptation that help them do this. Camels don't store water in their humps; instead they store fat, which can be broken down to produce energy and water when food and water are scarce. Their humps also help them regulate their body temperature by providing them with insulation. Their thick fur prevents them from getting sunburnt and helps them to keep cool. Some camels also have a thick layer of insulating fur that they shed in the summer months. It's not surprising then, that ancient camels have been found as far north as the Arctic circle, where their ancestors would have had to survive harsh winters in the snow.

WHY DID T. REX HAVE SMALL ARMS?

Tyrannosaurus rex is one of the most well known dinosaurs. With its powerful jaws and huge teeth it's easy to see why. But the arms of *T. rex* are shorter than you might expect for a predator.

Tyrannosaurs are famous for their disproportionately small arms. Yet these little limbs were surprisingly well muscled. Scientists are still unsure what they were used for, but theories have included a role in mating, feeding or in helping the animal stand up from a lying-down position. We now know that juvenile tyrannosaurs were much slimmer and more lightly built than the adults, with arms slightly more in proportion with the rest of their bodies. So perhaps tyrannosaurs used their arms to tackle prey when they were young. And as they grew up and developed massive heads and a bone-crunching bite, their arms became less important and simply stopped growing.

DID DINOSAURS NEED FEATHERS TO FLY?

When some dinosaurs started evolving wings, most began to form bird-like structures. So what do the bat-like wings of *Yi qi* tell us about the evolution of birds?

Towards the end of the Jurassic, about 160 million years ago, some smaller, feathered dinosaur species began to evolve wing structures very similar to modern-day birds. A famous example of this is *Archaeopteryx*, often referred to as the first bird. In 2007, research on a dinosaur called *Yi qi* discovered that it also had wings, but they were membranous ones, more like those of a bat. Scientists believe that *Yi qi* could glide from tree to tree like a flying squirrel, rather than using the flapping flight of birds. This is a really exciting discovery as it suggests that various wing forms evolved during the Jurassic, so there may potentially be other novel dinosaur wing forms waiting to be discovered.

CAN YOU GET DIFFERENT VEGETABLES FROM ONE PLANT?

Broccoli, Brussels sprouts, cauliflower and cabbage all look and taste very different when on a dinner plate. But how different are they really?

There is one special plant that has been used as a source of domesticated plants. This plant is *Brassica oleracea*, the wild mustard plant. Different parts of it have been cultivated and selected for different qualities – for instance, the terminal bud for cabbage, lateral buds for Brussels sprouts, the stem and flowers for broccoli, and the clustered flowers for cauliflower. All these varieties that you see and eat come from the same species, *Brassica oleracea*, and farmers are still looking into using it to produce new varieties.

HOW DO PEANUTS GROW?

From helicopters... to hooks, plants use very different strategies to disperse their seeds, but one of the oddest strategies is found in the peanut plant.

Most plants use water, wind or animals to distribute their seeds. Peanuts, however, are not among them. After a peanut flower is pollinated the flower wilts and curves down. It then starts growing downwards, pushing down into the ground and burying itself. Once it's in the ground, the peanut develops and grows. That's why peanuts are also called groundnuts. If it's not harvested, each seed – which is what we eat – grows into a new peanut plant and then the lifecycle starts again. This means the plant keeps its offspring close – it's the mother hen of the plants.

Peanuts don't grow on trees like other nuts. In fact, they aren't nuts at all but the underground seeds of a tropical legume plant related to peas and beans.

WHAT CAN SURVIVE A WILDFIRE?

Giant sequoias are some of the biggest trees in the world, with trunks measuring 9 m (30 ft) across and bark up to 90 cm (35 in) thick. What's the reason behind this extra thick coat?

A sequoia's thick bark can be very, very thick and full of tannic acid, which gives it its red colour and also helps it resist fires. This means that the small fires that occur in the Sierra Nevada, California actually don't hurt the sequoias. Instead they clear out the underbrush so sequoia seedlings can then have a clear place to grow, free of competition from other trees. Previous fire management regimes allowed the undergrowth to build up so that the fires that now happen in the Sierra Nevada are often much bigger and turn into wildfires. These wildfires can also damage the big trees and make it much less possible for the seedlings to grow.

HOW DO PLANTS KNOW WHEN TO GROW?

Sprouting, budding or flowering at the wrong time of year can be really damaging for a plant. If a seed starts developing in the middle of winter, the delicate seedling could freeze and die on a cold night. And if a plant blossoms before pollinators are around, it might never reproduce.

A bean plant seed germinates and grows in response to the right temperature and water content in the soil.

Plants have developed ways to tell when the right time is to do all these things. Some seeds, for example, need to go through a period of cold and wetness to germinate. These conditions tell the seed winter has passed and spring is just around the corner. The plant knows it is safe to start growing. This 'knowledge' is done at a genetic level, through proteins and genes that activate and deactivate depending on temperature and humidity. For wild plants, this happens naturally with the seasons. But if someone is trying to grow a seed in a greenhouse or in a foreign environment for the plant, they will have to recreate winter conditions and trick the seed by freezing it before planting it. Otherwise, the seed won't grow!

Crocus (opposite) are among the very first flowers to bloom each spring, and cowslip (above) is another early spring flower.

IS CORAL A PLANT OR AN ANIMAL?

Coral reefs are underwater ecosystems teeming with life. But what are these huge structures made of?

Corals may look like plants or rocks, but they're actually animals like you and me. Most corals start life as a microscopic larva, which swims around searching for a place to settle down. When it finds what it's looking for, it attaches itself to a surface and matures into a stationary form called a polyp. It then starts producing more identical polyps and secreting a hard skeleton around itself. As the colony grows, more and more skeletons get built on top of each other and eventually form the massive structure we know as a reef. Most of the colours of coral come from algae, which photosynthesize and produce nutrients for the coral. When a coral bleaches due to heat stress and pollution, it turns white and this is a signal that the corals have lost their algae and will struggle to find enough food to survive.

INDEX

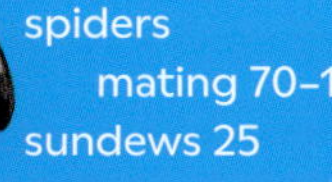

First published by the Natural History Museum, Cromwell Road, London SW7 5BD

ISBN 9781486317820

A catalogue record for this book is available from the National Library of Australia

This edition published exclusively in print only, in Australia and New Zealand, by:

CSIRO Publishing
Private Bag 10
Clayton South VIC 3169
Australia
Telephone: +61 3 9545 8400
Email: publishing.sales@csiro.au
Website: www.publish.csiro.au
Sign up to our email alerts: publish.csiro.au/earlyalert

Designed by
Fuszion, Rick Heffner

Reproduction by
Saxon Digital Services

Printed in China by
Toppan Leefung Printing Ltd.

Front cover: Penguin: ©Joey_Danuphol/Shutterstock
Back cover: Moon: ©Miguel Claro/Science Photo Library; Polar bear: ©T-Service/Science Photo Library; Jellyfish: ©scubadesign/Shutterstock; Beetle: ©Alex hyde/naturepl.com

PICTURE CREDITS

P.2 (chicken) ©Valentina_S/Shutterstock; (rabbit) ©Geza Farkas/Shutterstock; (chameleon) ©Jan Bures/Shutterstock; (jellyfish) ©scubadesign/Shutterstock; p.3 (moth) ©yamaoyaji/Shutterstock; (moon) ©gailhampshire/Flickr; (dolphins) ©Willyam Bradberry/Shutterstock; (reindeer) ©V. Belov/Shutterstock; (camel) ©Shengyong Li/Shutterstock; (sequoia) ©Lucky-photographer/Shutterstock; p.4 ©UniquePhotoArts/Shutterstock; p.5 ©Rudmer Zwerver/Shutterstock; p.6 ©Jamil Bin Mat Isa/Shutterstock; p.7 ©Valentina_S/Shutterstock; p.8 ©T-Service / Science Photo Library; p.8-9 ©Ondrej Prosicky/Shutterstock; p.9, 69 ©Power and Syred/Science Photo Library; p.10 (top) ©Joey_Danuphol/Shutterstock; p.10 (bottom)©Doug Allan/naturepl.com; p.11 ©Irina Kozhemyakina/Dreamstime.com; p.12 ©Kim Taylor/naturepl.com; p.15 ©aaltair/Shutterstock; p.16 ©Suzi Eszterhas/Minden/naturepl.com; p.18 (top) ©Jmaentz/Dreamstime.com; (middle) ©Four Oaks/Shutterstock; p.19 (top) ©milart/Shutterstock; (middle) ©©Geza Farkas/Shutterstock; (bottom) ©KanphotoSS/Shutterstock; p/20 ©Bubbers BB/Shutterstock; p.21 ©Adrian Davies/naturepl.com; p.22 (top) ©Pavel1964/Shutterstock; (bottom) ©Picture Partners/Shutterstock; p.23 ©Peter Scoones/naturepl.com; p.24 ©Norbert Wu/Minden/naturepl.com; p.25©Cathy Keifer/Shutterstock; p.26 (top) ©StanislavBeloglazov/iStock; p.27 ©Barry Mansell/naturepl.com; p.28 ©David Fleetham/naturepl.com; p.30 ©Darkdiamond67/Shutterstock; p.31 ©Jan Bures/Shutterstock; p.32 ©Claudio Contreras/naturepl.com; p.33 (top) ©Nick Garbutt/naturepl.com; (bottom) ©Hanne and Jens Eriksen/naturepl.com; p.34 ©Eric Baccega/naturepl.com; p.35 ©Franco Banfi/naturepl.com; p.36 ©Rajh.Photography/Shutterstock; p.37, 61 (bottom) ©Brent Stephenson/naturepl.com; p.38 (right) ©WildlifeWorld/Shutterstock; p.39 ©davemhuntphotography/Shutterstock; p.40 ©Juergen Freund/naturepl.com; p.41 ©scubadesign/Shutterstock; p.42 ©TRR/Shutterstock; p.43 (top) ©Reinhard Radke; (main) ©Jabruson/naturepl.com; p.44 ©Dr Richard Lee; p.45 (main) ©TigerStocks/Shutterstock; (bottom) ©Christophe Quintin/Flickr; p.46, 49 ©Solvin Zankl/naturepl.com; p.47 (main) ©University of Washington; NOAA/OAR/OER; (insert) ©NOAA Okeanos Explorer Program, Galapagos Rift Expedition 2011/Science Photo Library; p.48 ©Mike Veitch/robertharding.com; p.50 ©Jared et al., 2015, Current Biology 25, 2166–2170 August 17, 2015 ª2015 Elsevier Ltd All rights reserved http://dx.doi.org/10.1016/j.cub.2015.06.061; p.51 ©Mark Bowler/naturepl.com; p.52 ©Alex Hyde/naturepl.com; p.53 ©Nature Production/naturepl.com; p.54 ©yamaoyaji/Shutterstock; p.55©Stephen Dalton/naturepl.com; p.56, 57 ©Magnus Lundgren/naturepl.com; p.59 ©Noradoa/Shutterstock; p.60 ©Piotr Naskrecki/Minden/naturepl.com; p.61 (top) ©Alex Cooper Photography/Shutterstock; p.62-63 ©Wild Wonders of Europe/Aukan/naturepl.com; p.63 (top) ©©Willyam Bradberry/Shutterstock; p.64-65 ©Juan Gaertner/Science Photo Library; p.65 ©gailhampshire/Flickr; p.67 ©Miguel Claro/Science Photo Library; p.68 ©Julitt/Shutterstock; p.70 (insert)©Christopher Bellette/Dreamstime.com; p.70-71 ©Premaphotos/naturepl.com; p.72 ©Majna/Shutterstock; p.73 ©Milan Radisics/naturepl.com; p.74 ©Thomas Marent/Minden/naturepl.com; p.75 ©V. Belov/Shutterstock; p.76-77 ©Fred Bavendam/Minden/naturepl.com; p.77 ©HollyHarry/Shutterstock; p.78, 79 ©Mitsuaki Iwago/Minden/naturepl.com; p.80 ©Stephan Morris/Shutterstock; p.81 ©Maximillian cabinet/Shutterstock; p.82-83 ©Alex Tumee/Shutterstock; p.83 (top) ©Shengyong Li/Shutterstock; p.85 ©Emma Willoughby; p.86 ©Martin Fowler/Shutterstock; p.87 (top) ©shinja jang/Shutterstock; (bottom) ©nednapa/Shutterstock; p.88 ©Alexander Varbenov/Shutterstock; p.89 ©Lucky-photographer/Shutterstock; p.90 ©David Aubrey/Science Photo Library; p.91 (top) ©JIL Photo/Shutterstock; (bottom) ©Bruno Petriglia/Science Photo Library; p.92-93 ©Alex Mustard/naturepl.com

Every effort has been made to contact and accurately credit all copyright holders. If we have been unsuccessful, we apologise and welcome correction for future editions and reprints.